Brian Dennis Hartford

Where Her Ghosts Walks Still

A Collection of Poems

Namri'd
Publishing, LLC

Namri'd Publishing, LLC

2 Marietta Court Ste A #117
Edgewood, NM 87015

www.namridpublishing.com

ISBN-13: 978-0-9985432-8-4

First Printing: April 19, 2020

10 9 8 7 6 5 4 3 2 1

Printed in the United States of America

To my wife...1066.

Introduction

What are poems if not memories of the soul? A voice, speaking to a life once lived, now only fading images left to walk in the shadows of the mind so very real, so deeply set, that they can and do mold us, forge us into who we are as a person in the present weather we know this or not.

The following collection of poems is just that, fragments of past lives, as I see of them now. Many fleeting moments in dream or in waking. When I fully remember of who I was so long ago. In the reminiscing of past loves, those passings in good or bad. Still haunting in the hope of forgiveness, or in revelation perhaps, of the day when we will meet again.

Enjoy!

"What ghosts walk here…that memories cannot?"

Stoya Tepes Dracu

CONTENTS

The Stars Above Forever's Sea

We were once the stars above forever's sea

Ageless

Hopeful

Lost in our image as reflected below us in the pallid water's eave

Free to drift in ever dreaming

Oblivious to the dangerous depths and the drowning in God's grand illusion

Where, weightless, we sink

Slip from our own vision

Helpless, fragile little things

Terrified and clawing

Mouths open, screaming, desperate to our final pleads

Muted in the silence of the deep

Thick and strangling

Crushing

Until only the faintest memory lives in that one last momentary glimmer

Of when we had once been the stars above forever's sea.

In the Great Without

Here upon this place we've been unable to forget

Etched in our memories from the beginning set

We met for the first time

Just as the last time

As will be the next time

Upon some tower, under a moon, above the sea

To walk again in the dying garden

Whilst our image fades with each kiss

Soon to be as ghosts in the other's mind

And some phantom voice

Calling out inaudible among the ages of a love long gone
missing to the lie of time

But still bound in one solemn vow

To be forever as this; our image

A final parting reflection upon the iris of two souls forever in
passing, until the end of time.

Her Whisper is the Book I Wrote

Her words formed slowly

Careful of memory and its death

Her lips, red, wet, and wanting

Quietly reminiscing of love's dreadful story

Her heart's last beating

That sound; the echo of a last winter

When desperation fell dead in driving snows

A lifetime, bitter as the inking salt upon the love affair between pen and paper

Cruel and bound in the false promise of a wax seal

For such is the love affair of souls

A letter written, but never sent

Left unopened in the death of hope

And one last unfinished kiss.

The Need of Lust

It was in that moment, when

The night was still, yet

Its pulse raged, deafening

The sounds of sex drowning out all else

As we tore at soft flesh wanting of a deeper passion

To know of what it is to be loved

To feel what it was to be wanted.

And she slips from us, lifeless

A momentary need left curbside

A consummation of lusts cruelty

And the searching for the next pretty face.

In a Night Not So Long from Now

There is a night, not so long from now

When once tiny embers will make their way into a long-awaited inferno

When he will know the touch of our fingertips writing long unspoken desires upon his skin

Where once fleeting kisses find firmness in their demands

As outside, the storm still rages against us

Comforted in the sweet spiced candles that flicker softly upon our bodies lustful in black sheets, drowning

Our breath, caught unfinished, unable to fully take in or out in expectation

Drunk, in the quenching of our lust in the other

As our desires run free from the ages of us

As it was a thousand lifetimes ago

When we ran wild and uncaring of what a world thinks

Of when he kissed her and he kissed him as he kissed them

Unbound and fearless

In the memory of a night not so long from now.

Upon Our Meeting

We saw each other in passing through the windows of time

Our reflections never fully meeting

But long enough to know of the other's smile

The other's eyes

The other's soul

Then one day we did meet

And are still the strangers that we had always been.

An Invite to Dance
(My Vampire)

I see you there under a dark moon brooding

Amidst the Nightshades and Ivy blooming

A Lily's caress in the hand of temptation rest

Where upon the city gray you set

A final walk among past graves the test.

Time is translucent, unforgiving, unknowing

As your ages pass like granite in the wind blowing

Famished and wanting in the thirst

From under the lid and through time's dust.

Walk now beneath the candle-chandeliers showing

With a grand dress and ornamented eyes, fair faced, wet ruby
lips licking

To the call of midnight's last minutes whisper calling

The sound, my heart's last beating in the blood upon the floor.

Reveal now, to the world your story

Of the longing sadness in the castle winds warning

And the long dead count of seasons turning

Whilst a ghost ship freed drowns the sea, burning

Come! Let us dance this last midnight hour

Come! Let us feast upon those we desire

To love the end so soon dawning

For tonight you are the world's last knowing.

A Kiss is Everything and Nothing

We kissed

Expectantly

Each in the knowing that there will be an end to this

She spoke of long dead things and I tasted their flesh upon her lips

I saw the reflection of me in the distance of her gaze

A soon to be forgotten face.

And

I breathed

She breathed

We breathed

For the last breath of the living is the first breath of the dead

And with her lips firm upon mine

I knew then, that

"A kiss is everything, and nothing…"

A Walk Among Autumn's Tomb

It's time to walk again through Autumn's tomb

Where dreams are the birth of winter soon

To lament of spring and a picnic noon

Of a summer once, under the Parisian moon.

It's a quiet walk that I will take

To visit the smile which haunts me still in rest and wake

To drink again, the ivy cold, and wait

To dream of an old romance, our fate.

Soon, I'll hold the hand that held my own

Which pulled me from the River Seine so cold

Wrest me from the death I sought

And forged a love which time still wrought.

For I still kiss the lips of Autumn's bloom

For this night, she had died in winter's womb

Wrested from an eternal doom

Her gift to me, a hundred Junes.

And here, again, I find in this

Her smile still, as when we first kissed

Left untouched upon the stone

Awaiting me, my Autumn's Winter coming home.

The Day When

I know the day when I will lose your touch from mine

The last time when our hands will hold the other's

Our last kiss, which will linger burning upon our lips forever wondering

Left again to searching in the place where parched hearts languish, desperate

As your image recedes from me

In the final parting of our souls.

And so, here and now

While in the flesh

While still yet young enough and beautiful

Let us love with a raging in our hearts

And a burning so deep it consumes the stars

While we set to conspire against every second in the passing hours

Unbridled, but forewarned of our end.

For I know when the day will come

When I will lose your touch from mine

For my heart speaks of it often

Of the very moment when

Feeble and no longer able

We break

As if some last ray of sunlight straining before the utter dark in its final exhale

Where once sweet dreams turn bitter sweet

In the domino of memories

And the prophetic words of *"Till death do us part"* find its full circle

Where, in some nightstand drawer, an old photo of me turns sepia

And beyond, a home once in garden, now deserted, decays

And my hand painted heart upon the door slowly peels away, but still welcoming

In a testament for others whom might still wish to tell you of the love we had.

And I let slip your hand from mine…because I loved you.

And I will let slip my hand of yours…because I still love you.

Kiss Away Forever

We kiss

With eager lips

Teeth tearing

Our tongues

The branding

Left to scar, deep and everlasting

Forged in the fires of our deceptions

Where all the wanting of a world slips into its final dying under a universe with all its stars falling

And a lonely God left crying

As the ocean of time recedes from us

Exposing desert shores, thirsty and dying

So, to this

In this

We kiss

With tongues black from the poison of the lie

Two dead hearts soon to be silent, in the hopeful death of the promise

That we could still, just maybe, kiss away forever.

It Was There in the Rain in the Sea

It was there in the rain in the sea

Beneath the mangrove trees

Amidst the life-giving waters that welled up hopeful

We kissed

As thunder called out into the darkening sky to a world deaf to all but the moment of our hearts

Where lightening flashed upon the backs of obsidian sea-spiders set in their poisonous ways

Turning them for a moment into diamonds upon raindrop pearled necklaced webs

Though our love was unafraid of their deception

And, where, we knew the hearts of the silver fish racing desperate against the receding tide

For it was there, in that place

We were as one against a failing world

And knew the truth of it

That it was us slipping away from them

And not them from us

And, in that moment, we longed suddenly

To drown there

To die beneath the cliffs in a tormented sea

Pulled out and away with the tide

To be one with the souls of the silver fish, racing

Out past the reef into the coming storm

To be pushed under by fierce waves

Let life slip from us as does the sand into the gray depths below, unafraid

For it was there in the storm under the mangrove trees

Behind the veil of poisonous spider webs

Amidst the broken rain drop circle reflections of our entwined image

We kissed

As the rain became the sea again.

Left Lost, in the Quenching of our Thirst

We danced

Wet, in the heat of a provocative rhythm

To a voice calling out in the neon strobe light-flashing

To lust

Her reflection caught in the glistening beads of sweat that trace down and around our bodies, wanting

The scent of her perfume upon salted skin, plunging us unhesitant into the chasm of hunger to crash as waves upon the rocks

As our bodies become one in new prospects with lips upon lips upon lips and tongue upon tongue upon tongue

Seduced in the taste of cigarettes and honey gin

Our blood, unable almost

Labored in the speaking of sinful prospects from daring mouths

Our image, framed silent against the film of the world

A most beautiful stop motion animation playing out upon the iris

In shadowed tones of flesh on flesh on flesh

Desirous

And it was there in low-pulse light-flash warnings that we fell away from the world

Left lost, in the quenching of our thirst of our reflections kissed away in the sweat upon her skin.

And if I Were to Die Today

And if I were to die today

I would leave this one thing behind to you

My heart, in the flesh

So that you will know always, the beating of it

Its ever-burning fire

To remind you of the moment when our eyes first met

In the doom of the setting sun

When the stars and moon still set out to play above the Night
Phlox bloom and fireflies dreaming

As we retire to cool white linen sheets to know of each other,
our coming life

Now only your life, and what it still can be

As I wait from the other side for you and you alone.

Yes

I will leave to you my heart, the flesh of it upon my death

So that its slow wistful beating will lull you to sleep amidst
life's tempest storms that you must still face, alone

To guide you when you are lost

Back to our sacred place

To make you smile when memories turn sad

To laugh with you in the best of times still ahead

To assure you of the love we will always have

Despite this temporary parting.

Yes, this is the one thing

My heart will remain in the flesh

Beating strong and fearless

As the thunder calling from beyond the veil

A near inaudible whisper beating; *"My Love...my love...my love..."*

And so, it is that I slip to my eternal slumber

Gone from any other to know, but you

My flesh, as it dissolves to dust

Save only for my heart still beating ever after upon the mausoleum stone

Echoing forth from my chamber to the sound of my one and only promise;

To love, forever, you...my love.

My Death is Where the Stars Rest

There is a death in your thoughts

A burning in my mind of you

The image

A tempest's smile

Your whisper as it thunders low but steady, building into a scream that soon shatters the universe into a trillion shards of glass

For the stars are of your making

Forged from my fire for you

And, there too, the black in between them

My death shroud, woven from your indifference

And I smile wanton still

For what is my death anyways

But the velvet pillow of my soul upon where your stars rest.

Reflections

And we pass as ghosts

Reflections upon the window

Washed away by indifferent rains

The image of our last goodbye.

In the Sound of Melting Snow

In the sound of melting snow

Fast running

I hear your tears

The sound of them falling soft upon the world

Frozen and mournful

A never ending white in the edge of silence

Save for the faintest trickle deep beneath, finding its way

Soon to rage again as the river once did in spring

As we had, barefoot and running

Careful that no minute left us wanting in the chasing of our
dreams

There upon the high meadow

In the laughter of mountain Iris and Honeysuckle

Beneath impassible peaks and the treacherous gorge

Where, in the sound of melting snow

We had come to know the final calling of our souls.

We Still Yet May Die of It

And my lips still feel her kiss from across time

A place so far away from me now

Of barren dust and drowning rains

Where beast and man are nearly indistinguishable from the other

And there, amidst the chaos of the grasses

Past the smothering jungle where the roar of kings still echo in gunshot politics

We could

For a brief moment

Slip away into the dream of only us

Hidden away in the thick of night

Beyond known stars where her goddess moon resides

And my Southern Cross cannot see

Where, our souls found love as we ran from what they would have of us.

And now, in a hundred years from that place

Her kiss still haunts me

Burns my soul like the iron did upon her skin

And the whip upon my back

Awakening me from quinine drenched dreams to scream out past the tent flaps of my bedroom

Sweating

To the naked image of us under a night sky

To be what the sun and moon are still forbidden to be

And we loved unafraid of consequence

Of death

Of the truth that to this day, we still yet may die of it.

Remembering What Fireflies Bring

She didn't know you could catch fireflies in your hand

Hold them and make a wish upon them

Then set them free

To watch them rise into the night sky to be as the stars.

And, there amongst the Willow trees and a murmuring stream

Beyond the rose guarded gates of our keep

The scene; as reflected in the poison glistening upon the grass

She whispers her final wish and sets us free

With the hope that we can be as the fireflies

And live as stars again.

The Death of Time is a Love Ever Waiting

Upon the winds of time

Our thoughts call out in search of each other

Desirous, in memories struggling to live again

Tumbling like fragile glass upon the tempestuous shores of
eternity

Where

We

Wait upon bridges

Wait upon a giant's causeway and shadowed towers

Upon a wall ever crashing into the sea

Sentinel to the passing of moons and stars ever dying

For there, in these places, our souls remember the time when
our love was reckless as the waxen wings of Icarus reaching
for the sun

His feathers falling back from the heavens in torrents as arrows
upon my armor in my need for you.

And now

Here again

In this moment

We hold hands hopeful in the last of our moments

Gleeful against the coming storm

For time runs from us

Like the river in the canyons below

Flush with rage in its aimless searching

Jealous and lustful as the blood upon the flowered grasses in an endless battle with mystical masked faces from some distant and dreadful shore come to take you

Again

And in this, our final defiant daring

Hand in hand

We can so boldly laugh at the lances charging before us

Because we know

Don't we

That times greatest enemy

Is a love content in ever waiting for the other.

In the Death of Heather

I long to know the touch of you again

Your sweet scent upon the Highland winds

To know the pressing of my body upon yours

To trace your face

Your curves in a flowery dress

Upon a hill

Waiting in the warm spring breezes

Your eyes were such a deep blue

Which made the sun smile

Dreaming and wistful of a time when we would make our break from here and run barefoot across the world

In search of better dreams

A life to make our own

But now

There is only the freezing winds of winter

Clawing and tearing

Fast blowing once better times from us

As your tears become the falling snow

Fast frozen upon blood drenched fields, blanketing once beautiful Heather

Beneath, the green grass withers

And once soft earth turns to stone

As time's hammer shatters swords and armor upon the anvil of hope

A sound so unearthly in its final silence

An ever ringing of the chessboard when all the pieces have fallen

Broken soldiers

Now, only discarded statues upon the ground

Stone faced and praying up to indifferent gods

Unable to weep but in memories alone

Motionless hearts wanting of forgiveness

Unable even, to whisper a last prayer

Left now, long forgotten ghosts still marching

Still advancing upon long empty fields

In faithful steadfast formations

Reliving some old Saga no longer ever spoken

Amidst dusty bones

And aged headstones

Beneath an old bridge in Stamford

My soul, but one of many

Whom had found their love

In the death of Heather.

Rings in the Snow

I trace your face

The image left in my mind of you

Feel your breath in the evening winds

Where your scent ligers still within my bed

As the ceiling above seems to fade away

Becoming a black and timeless place

My body paralyzed in linen sheets

White as a frozen sea

Swallowing

The image of your eyes

Of you dancing

Fading fast

My only hope

The smile

The laugh

The look you had

That day we met on icy shores

Lost so far away

My promise then to cross the oceans

To sail far away

Into the stars

To live on new worlds

To be the one

The only one

And now your gone

Just a ghost

A sliver of light left to linger

For me to trace my finger upon

An outline in the dark of you

Dancing still upon the ice of my frozen heart

Fading as our rings in the snow had

Becoming artifacts distant and falling

As does your memory through the ages of me

My tears, become the falling snow

The blizzard at the end of time

And I fall fast asleep

Dreaming again of a day I might see you there

Upon some distant shore

Your soul as it was is in the sunlight

Warming me

Filling me with hope

And a life we still may get to live

Together

When I kiss away your whispers

In the promises of forever

And a love never dying

Still fearful

In the image of two rings fast fading away in the snow.

Than Any had Expected

It was her way

Strong, silent, indifferent to the world

Walking bold

Upon the line between life and death

Her soul was Africa.

And she knew how to suffer

For it was the world's way then

Her way always

For most any there

Though, perhaps, we chose not to see it.

And so, we loved

Labored to find our resolution amidst the horrors

Driven to find a refuge from it

Entwined

Beneath the stars

Under endless skies

Amidst the grasses

Within the feasts of feasts.

And it was there in Africa

There, amidst the just barely surviving

That we lived for a moment longer

Than any had expected.

Of Butterflies and Super Novas

Upon green flowered fields

She chases butterflies

Under blue skies where the red hawks fly

Circling without care to the world below

Indifferent to time and the passings of man.

She delights in feel of them

Their fragile wings within her hands

Trusting

The fluttering tongue-kisses upon her cheeks

Laughing

She sets them free into the winds above.

And under a fading sun she grew

A woman amidst the locusts of a decaying world

Illuminated in the coming of death she runs

Fearless and with conviction into it

A single focused vision.

And there from our doorway

Beyond the endless fires

Before an army

She rides

Fearless

Her hope in the knowing that one day, she will feel the kiss of butterflies again.

She Walks Dark Streets

She walks alone in dark streets

Through geometric cut shadows of a lost place

Amused by the sounds of a slow dying

For what is forever anyways.

Her face veiled from the world

Save for a slight smile

Illuminated by the soft glow of a cigarette

Indifferent to the cat-calls and honking horns

To the filth flowing down into the drains

Indifferent to the promise of God's love in the sign above

For what is forever anyways.

She stands naked before him

Pale white bones colored in part by the late-night glow of
television sex

And the faltering neon signage just beyond the broken window
which read, "Cocktails"

And he kisses her with all the passion that is his aimless
desperation

His mouth fumbles upon her breasts

She smiles kindly, helpful in his nursing

For what is forever anyways.

And there upon the floor of desperation he lay

The ashes of a last cigarette, fading

Its embers caught momentary lifting in a last exhale

And she smiles contemplative

For what is forever anyways, to anyone?

She knows of the world.

In the Fall of Leaves

It is in the fall of leaves

Still young in their red and amber hues

Their eagerness to tumble dead upon still green grasses

That we know the dying of the world is upon us again

And, what is that sound?

The scratching they make upon the cold ground, blowing

Is it that of our nails clawing at the insides of our coffins?

Trapped deep in the forgotten earth

Where, our lives give way slowly to the veil of dream

Hour by hour

Whence, fondly, we remember when we once walked upon summer shores, barefoot

And swam in warm waters

While sand castles stood towering

Echoing of grander things amidst the glow of bonfires

Now left to ruin and a gray death slowly eroding

Out and down into a sullen place where even starfish have no power

For winter has come

And will remain always even if just a as a sliver in our hearts

A dark and desolate place

Temporary, but forever in its haunting

Gnawing upon the soul

Cold and savage

For there is no mercy for any but the longing leaves of Fall

For only they know, that in surrendering they will set free

Free to roam as the winds dictate of them, and with little other care

To know not sadness, but only possibility

To surpass the trappings of other living things

The long dead flower left to hang upon the noose of its own stem

Of little living things, desperate in the pursuit of a warm place

Of the stream now but dripping ice when once it raged fast and full

Or of the lonely heart of a woman and a last Christmas in a faltering marriage

Her children long gone and living new lives

And a husband never home.

So, it is, in these things, that I long dream to be as the leaves of Fall

Free and ever drifting

A ghost in the death of the world

Aimless, but all knowing

For death will come despite a yearning soul

And I scratch upon my coffin lid…the image of a leaf, drifting…

To Speak as the Stars

And I wish to speak as the stars do

To tell of the slow dying

The slipping of the glass from the silver

Reflections left wanting in old photos fast fading

A diary perhaps

The bucket list

Pages upon pages of penned hopes gone unread and unbound

But still; a promise to ourselves of what might have been

If only we could have

For time grips us with a firm hand, crushing and relentless

As the sea in the deepest depths

The earth in the grave

Or the gaze of the stars above, upon us, ever judging

Without any mercy

A constant reminder of what we have long forgotten

That life is only but the reflection we give to it

And that we ourselves, also

Are the reflection of what the stars had dream of themselves.

The Forbidden Kiss

There, in a secret place

Known to us only

I kiss the rain from your lips

As lightening danced across your face

Your eyes, momentary stars, wicked and knowing

As I could feel the storm in you

Just under the surface of your soul

A ghostly skin

Lost to any form, save for what the light of the moon gives it

The shadows of it, seductive

Drawing me into your dark desires

A failing of love, perhaps

But lustful in its wanting of salvation

A wanting so deep

An absolute need.

And she sleeps not so far away in our darkened room

With doors shut and curtains drawn to the world

Her knowing

While, here

With you in my arms

My mouth upon yours

My heart lost, beating relentless

Amidst the garden of sin, in the rain

Just beyond her window

I fall lustful

Drowning amongst the roses

And to the taste of the ivy-rain upon you

Trickling down into your sex, where

My tongue following, needful

And as if in prayer upon my knees a penance of the Thornberry

I drink, and drink, and drink my fill of you

Whilst, above

You lord yourself over me, my weakness

And smile disregarding of my want

For I am but a momentary thing to you

A passing in the night of a million nights

And I kiss, and I drink lustful

And you laugh

For I know too the taste of my wife upon you also

Saw her smile content in her sleep

And knew then

That you are our one forbidden kiss.

Under Long Dead Stars

And, under long dead stars, we kiss

Still

Their deaths, the fuel of the fire in our hearts

Burning ever greater in our love

As the centuries passed through our souls

Racing to a known end

Which only the moon knows, perhaps

Or the sun, maybe

Our blood within, yes

And, well

There will be many "ANDs" now, won't there?

For we are, you and me, the great "AND"

For that is our love story, the never ending of the word "AND"

The truth that, amidst the inevitable death of stars

And the passing of time

When, moons rise their last rise

And suns shine their last light

And earths breathe their last breaths

That there is more to us, then in any other thing but "AND"

For we are the final curtain-call-kiss under long dead stars.

A Night Once, Long Ago in Babylon

Our eyes meet long ago in a strange place not yet known to me

There among a new city set by the river

Where, upon it, flowers of all sorts grew hanging

And fresh fruits were plentiful

I felt the dust in my throat and the harsh sun beating down
upon me

The smell of rotting meat laden with preserving spices and
stale mead-wine.

The calls of street side venders and beggars deafened me as
they fought for my attention

My horse whinnied and stamped in protest upon the dirt streets
as camels bellowed under their miserable burdens, and
incessantly hungry flies

All was this amber color with little distinction between what or
who, or why even

Made dreamlike by the stark, rich colors of freshly dyed linens
blowing gently high above

And there, past the unsettled scene I saw her

Beautiful atop the highest balcony of raised gardens in a place
still called Babylon.

And, even now, in this future city of order and concrete, she
visits in my dreams

Bringing the desperation of that place

As I awake suddenly choking from the dust and rank where there is none

Her eyes still peering at me from beyond the veil of time, taunting, as in our first meeting.

And I have found, if I lay motionless

I can know the way she felt upon me in that night

Still

The scent of her skin, it's perfume; that of the dying rose

And I can still taste her sweat, dripping upon me like some bitter honey, thick and oppressive

Her eyes, deep and endless as the night sky awash in a brilliant violet hue ever gleaming

Beneath, on perfect lips, an arrogant taunting smile rested

For she owned the world from there, I knew then

As she does now of this world also.

And I exhale in the lifting of her body from mine

That breathless moment between dream and death

And what her lips speak now as they did to me then;

"What is forever anyways, but some night long ago in Babylon…"

Until We Sleep Again

She is the place I go

So far from me in the depth of dream

Her face all but a ghost now

A promise ever burning

Ever calling

Drawing me to where I can finally rest

There, amidst the nightshade and honeysuckle

Under a full moon

Where beyond lay sorrowful stars

Ever watching

As the vampire bats dance above the circling wolves below

Ever hungry

Amidst the rising embers of our fire

Ever hopeful as if tiny hearts seeking to burn

As do our shadows before the flames

Two bodies lustful in the raging of the world

Where the blood flows

Wild and wanting

Where a first kiss will be a last kiss

Our naked bodies already fast fading

As if tears in the sea

Lost

Left swimming, desperate

Until we sleep, again.

My Helen of Troy

From walls so high, that the sun could never fully rise

Just beneath the stars

Her eyes still meet with mine

Amidst last promises

Inaudible to the war drums thunder

Drown out in the promise of coming rain

Caught up like the winds through freshly red-dyed silk veils

Blowing, as will the blood of the conquered from beyond the sea.

And from the dead sand

Once bloomed white roses

Proud, now broken

Left to wither in the shadows of betrayal

To drown in a flood of black tears

Within their poisoned vases.

And there just beyond walls so high the sun could not rise

Just beneath the stars that no longer shine

Her eyes still meet with mine

Deceptive whispers still promising

In the whistling of a million red-dyed silk fletched arrows

Upon the rows and rows of poisoned black-glass vases breaking.

And to this I still wake, screaming

The sweat cutting through the dust of memory

Her face upon the ramparts, knowing

That the smell of freshly fallen corpses

Was all for you

My Helen of Troy.

Forget Me

It was when you had forgotten me

The last of my footsteps faded forever in the drifting snows

When all had fallen silent from the sound of your knife
withdrawing from the wound

The exiting steam, the last shadow cast of my memory

Left to dissipate into the sunlight, carried away by cold winds

That I could, in that moment

Know how to forgive you.

And it was there in that vision of the snow, kneeling

Blood soaked and sparkling

As I felt the last warmth of your skin, slipping

That you would know that I will still dream of you

For it was in when you have long forgotten me

That my love for you could finally set you free.

The Greatest Love Affair

What love affair they must have

The rain upon the window pain

As they move across the other, tracing down

The sensual lingering

The thoughtfulness of their touch

Caught up in an age of longing

Kept ever parted by a jealous sun.

Footsteps Upon the Dune

The desert falls from us, as the sand in the hour glass

Under a torturous sun

Drawing us, ever closer to our deaths

For we were Bedouin, once

Fearless and searching in the desolation of the Mecca

Our only testament, that of fading footsteps which spoke little
of our passing

And none of our going

Save perhaps what time may wish to remember of us

Our spirits, now but unanswered prayers

In the quiet crackle of sage fires under black tents

When the night winds blew gentle across ancient sands where
once mighty mountains stood

Now only ruin

Where above, the Shabria moon beckons to the stars

Their image, naked in the well water

For only the sun will ever truly know of us, our hearts

It is as our blood

A fire for a soul, and vengeful in its relentless quest to know
the ends of the world

Where the key to the past remained lost

Left hostage in the cost of want

And its ululation in the passing of our footsteps fast fading upon the dune.

As Diamonds

We were as diamonds, once

Forged from our love and ever burning

And we close our eyes, as our lips part kissing

Dreaming as the diamond does in the death of stars.

Of Cities Long Lost to Man

I still walk the streets of cities long lost to the heart of man

Hear the sounds of my footsteps echo lonely upon the cobblestone

Where the wind whispers of long past dreams

When the hands of men made beautiful things

And there was peace in words and in the heart.

But soon, our ambitions grew

And old Gods were replaced with new Gods

While theo-technocracy replaced once nobler thoughts for greed and war

And in a single flash, only ashes now lay, where once was hope.

And I walk, still, silent under a sorrowful moon

My ghosts shadow fading bit by bit

Until only its soul remains

Left to dream of once greater things

And a world long gone from the heart of man.

Beyond Strange Stars

Beyond strange stars, I dreamt

Of a place far from here where

She lay asleep upon a world of living, breathing machine

Her life near motionless to the pulse below her

The industrial rumblings and turnings of an evolution still not done in the making

Above, a sky where neither sun nor moon shown

But instead, only the endless fluorescent light of industry mined from soon to be dead stars.

I trace her face, her body,

The rise and fall of her chest ever so slight as she breathes

A low, peaceful, calculated, but unoccupied breath

A temperature flat and cold for there is no fire within save for only for the pre-programmed chemically initiated autonomic reflex of her system

I feel her pulse, strong, but devoid of any passion

The emollient of plasma infused oil coursing through carbon pex-line veins pumping away just beneath her waxy silicone, fiber meshed lined skin

Pushed through, by a heart beating slow and steady powered by the rhythm of muscle infused plastic valve devices, pumping in a synchronous manner, of its own mechanical timing, as if counting down to something

What, I could not know.

Beyond her

Lay a vast and seemingly endless coil of flesh and metal and plastic, writhing as if in the agony of birth

A new city, perhaps

With others as her, suspended and waiting

Looking blankly to the heavens as she does

A megapolis of such vast scope with no horizons

No up nor down

A place mechanically alive but nature-less, emotionless.

It moves autonomous of universal interaction, as if some undead newborn crawling, slipping, grinding away at something, the womb of time itself, perhaps

And all throughout

Rivers of oil and gas and refuse streamed below in deep chasms of pipes and fittings and all manner of cable and conduit into a putrid sea, deep and poisonous.

I look upon her, with infatuation

Her muted flesh and silent indifference

I move to kiss her upon deadpan lips

Desiring, if for no other reason but to remember something;

The taste of a flesh so not unlike my own

That of the sweet chemicals, and the faint noxious carbon exhale of her breath

I peer into her face, her eyes just under thinly veiled latex-like eyelids, for some form of feeling of presence, her soul maybe

But it was, and is if, looking instead into the black abyss between the stars

And I knew then in that dead place of her

That here amidst the grey and black and colorless veil they wait, she waits, as I wait

Suspended in neither life, nor death, nor dream, but oblivion

Statues peering outwards with sleeping eyes

Searching with an ambivalence and a relentless patience unknown to us, for what is time to them, I somehow instinctively know.

And upon my awakening from this nightly dream, her image fast slipping from my mind into the cool, crisp night of this earth

Where the city lights are still not greater than the stars

And all is natural and mortal

I breathe out gasping, for I am in that moment struck numb in the reason that my dream was not a dream,

But the memory of her within me, of a life not long from now

When our world had succumbed to the evolution of the machine and all is but nearly dead

A time when, we have long become immortal through science and chemistry

But mortal, still mortal, in the one thing we could not own, nor control, our souls.

And it is then, in that still of night

In the low hum of the city beyond my window

That I knew that I was her

As they are

As we already have become

Long dead bodies patiently waiting, for our souls to one day return.

In Black Waters

With a final breath and a fond farewell

Long fallen upon the deaf ears of lesser ghosts

I sink into black waters

To pass with others of my kind

Joining in that silent place

Where dreams are said to live, unending

Even as time erases all memories of our being.

There, in the black

Suspended in an endless deep

Weightless

My heart can finally speak its last wish

Only to vanish upon the fading concentric circle ripples above

Where shadows of love still dance oblivious

To our want of it.

Down in the forever of the deep

Our dreams come crushing

Relentless and cruel

A drowning in the drowning

Of the image of what we were supposed to do

But lacked the courage then to do

My last wish, drifting in the waves crest above long washed
away.

Fearless, In the tides below

Let us think of the time once

Where

Under the Caprian moon

We had found that we were free of our past, present, and future

Our worries, and the pains of living a life we did not want anyways

Where life became the dream, and the dream had but found us just only living to live it

Where upon the rocks below, our souls could slip away into the sea of the world

Never to be heard from again

As so many had before us

It is said.

And upon that stage

High above

Where the rocks stand as knives

Silver in the night

Where, as shadows we can still live

Our story

Playful voices in the winds of Punta Tragara, calling

A grand love reminiscing

Of a last time

When the wine bled its last drop into our empty glass

Like memory into the crashing waves below

Swept way to feed a grander memory

Where now only, we are but reflections

As lover's past, present, and future

Faces in the moonlight ripples upon the sea

Endless

Haunting

Calling

Seductive

Echoes

Our fateful reminder

To a time once, when, not so long ago

Death found the truth of us, fearless

And eternal

In the tides below.

Where Her Ghost Walks Still

She let slip, her hands from mine

To fall back upon the bleeding sunrise

Before an army

Bent on destruction

To the river Argeș, below

Her image, fast fading

A wingless angel

To ten thousand torches

To the cruelty of false ideology

And the lie which burns in my heart still

Left forever, to tear at the ages

Searching.

And from upon my tower, in the late of night

I wait in deep dreaming for her return

Haunted in the sound of her body, falling

The rush of the sweet morning air unable to keep her aloft

That sound of her, in the final resolution, echoing

When death caught her upon the rocks below

And her soul found its freedom, from me.

And, still, under morning stars

Soon to fade in the coming light

As a million nights have

And million more will

My hands clasp tightly, anxious

To the memory of hers in mine

That final moment

Where, my heart still strains to hear her last words

Long lost upon ancient winds

To remember the taste of her final tears

To savor that last kiss from her lips

Fearful and trembling

Lingering, and ever torturous

My soul forever wrapped in the shroud of an unforgiving god

Bound to an ageless nightmare calling

Unmerciful in the rushing water

Where her ghost walks still.

The Author

Brian Dennis Hartford is a published author and writer of fiction. He has a Bachelor's degree in Security Management with a focus on Terrorism Studies and has worked in the private security industry. He currently resides in the beautiful state of New Mexico, a land, a people, a culture, of which he draws much inspiration.

Available Now from Namri'd Publishing

Set in the near future, **Task Force 2198: A Memoir of War and the Second Revolution** is an uncompromising, gritty look into the lives of Benjamin and Lena Bradford who fight as shadow warriors in the world's most powerful Private Military Security Corporation, Paradigm. As America and the world plunges into economic and political chaos, they are driven by an unknown fate, the desire to hold onto the life they are slowly losing, and patriotism for a country they love. They take up arms to fight for an ideal that may no longer exist.

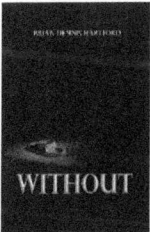

"What is forever anyways..."
Ianthe Gold is a Vampire who will do anything to save her one true love, Charlotte Bell Aberdeen. To finally be united with that one soul she has been chasing over the millennia, through time, space and across many worlds. But God as always, has other plans.

In **Rambled Thoughts**, Lee'Ann Imel-Hartford explores her inner self and her thoughts on eternity, transporting us through centuries of soul travel, the elements, and life. Take the journey with her as she explores her soul's travel through time and space in the search for her twin flame.

A Special Thanks

To friends and family who support my endeavors. To Unsplash for the great, free artwork! To Peter Murphy and Bauhaus for years of inspiration. To my Uncle Sam, my father's best friend and fearless poet of the high seas, may our souls meet once again. To Blvck Ceiling, and especially Fraunhofer Diffraction and their song "Affection" which found the right tone to close this project out. And last, but furthest from least, to my eternal whisper in the dark.

To Marilyn Raupfer, in memory and inspiration for the poem "In the Sound of Melting Snow". My memory of you will always be that of stories, life, and love. Thank you for being my friend. May we meet again beyond the veil.

Cover Photo Source Credits

◼ Unsplash

Namri'd

Publishing, LLC

www.ingramcontent.com/pod-product-compliance
Lightning Source LLC
Chambersburg PA
CBHW021204020426
42331CB00003B/191